JENNIFER E

C000262388

The Grief of The Sea

BROKEN SLEEP BOOKS

Published 2020,
Broken Sleep Books:
Cornwall / Wales

brokensleepbooks.com

First paperback Edition

Lay out your unrest.

Publisher/Editor: Aaron Kent
Editor: Charlie Baylis

Typeset in UK by Aaron Kent

Broken Sleep Books is committed to
a sustainable future for our planet,
and therefore uses print on
demand publication.

brokensleepbooks@gmail.com

ISBN: 978-1-913642-04-4

Contents

'...both ships and sea were things that broke to pieces.'

The Grief of The Sea

Jennifer Edgecombe

Bryan Wynter's 'Landscape, Zennor'

The dark is the sea that has soaked through,
dripping into buckets already full –
night-time in the day;
the granite blackened, the fields dimmed,
the moon in each headlight.
With each stroke of the paddle,
you tried to keep time with the sea –
the blue pulling you deeper
into the undertow. In the gallery,
my small body of water
rests in front of your canoe:
your final form, unmoored.

Bred in the Stone

after Vanishing Cornwall *by Daphne Du Maurier*

Half wondering and half afraid,
she carries her child to Madron Well

in the footsteps of the Earth Mother –
over hill tops and in groves

the granite rocks and stones are her handiwork –
a journey on foot lasting two days.

More power than prayer, she dips him
three times underneath the sun

and then once more until she believes
the baby is cured.

Grant

Our tour guide, an ex-miner –
his photo from thirty years ago
on the commemorative wall.

I always wanted to come back.
'THE END 16/2/90' painted on a locker,
tea urn still plugged in.

At seventy feet down he stopped us,
talked about depth,
then pulled a piece of ore from his pocket –

extracted from the lode a mile out to sea,
containing eighty percent tin.
This is worth more than gold and I will never let it go.

The Headland of Carbis Bay

is a corner of sedimentary rock
never quite exposed enough
to be walked around.

The sea rushes forward to remove footprints,
forcing walkers
up the emergency rope path.

From this height I have an overwhelming view
of home, refurbished with the orange of this sunset,
the day sliding down my bedroom wall.

I sit with binoculars at low tide searching
for traces of Bessie, Cintra, Vulture, Hampshire,
four wrecks laid down in one night, November 1893.

I see small black dots that could be anything.

Zennor Churchyard

archives the lost
Pool, Nance
craftsman, scholar
a laminated photograph, wildflowers

inside, a model schooner
remembers the lost at sea
Procter in the Pacific –
and those we'd walked across, under the grass

The Penlee Lifeboat Disaster

I

well they're mostly fishermen
they come from the same village as what I do
this is just a part-time job

I'm pretty lucky here
the sons of Mousehole
top notch

darts had just started
everyone was drinking laughing joking
a strange note in the wind

I asked him when he'll be round the corner
we call Land's End the corner
he said about just after tea

he said it was rolling a bit
a marker on the radar
slowly drifting in towards land

II

when the maroons were heard
stopped what they were doing
rushed to the station
only eight hands were needed

all dressed
the best he had
just sort of waited
waited and waited

and waited
to catch the right moment
to knock her off the slope
she went down and was gone

some thirty foot in height
like being in a washing machine
bouncing significantly
the ocean was very confused

III

a mother two children
eight miles east of Wolf Rock
together for Christmas
engines have stopped

     about fifty-foot seas

with water in the fuel tank
he was drifting faster than he thought
it was getting very difficult
less than a mile from shore

     sixty maybe seventy-foot waves

how very clean and new
the green painted deck looked

           extraordinary
           screaming
           bright pink court shoes

The Union Star was on her maiden voyage
The Union Star was the latest one

With the Union Star so close to shore
The Union Star was heading straight toward

I could see the helicopter and I could see the Union Star
Water getting into the engine of the Union Star

Solomon Browne went up onto the Union Star
But after sliding off the deck of the Union Star

        she was effectively out of the water
        two boxing bags
        trying to steady themselves
        throwing lines over
        shadows of people running
        it appeared they were just jumping

and the lifeboat crew were out
with their arms out

IV

he always seemed to be a free spirit
like a breath of air

she went out
and she's still out

Godrevy Lighthouse

I try to line up his painting
with the contours of the cliff

but a face changes over time –
rocks sliding down into the middle of the beach,

receding marram grass,
the edge unstable.

At least the lifeguard hut,
no longer in use but standing.

His route is now a memory –
the only other thing of his I own.

Newly marked: a desire line,
leading to the light.

Stunt Show Season

At this time of year posters
advertising the travelling show
appear in shop windows:

HERNE BAY;
EASTBOURNE;
I remember attending in HAYLE.

I have a photo of my brother
leaning over the crowd barriers
signing his stage-name for a fan: *Fandango!*

But leaves fall earlier than we expect
and as the posters disappear
it's hard to believe we had a summer.

elastic bands

my brother died with elastic bands in his pocket 15 of them
yellow or green small hoops for banding daffodils together
my mum has kept them since in a plastic pot with a red screw
lid that we used to keep drawing pins in or other stationary
when I was young she wrapped five around her pocket diary
and uses the others rarely last week one flew off across the
lounge and I watched her crawl on the carpet eventually she
found it intact not snapped still the same small yellow circle
perhaps he would have stretched one out into a bigger circle
deep inside his pocket with his thumb and forefinger while he
was bored or talking to someone

Daffodil

there's always one
daffodil
that doesn't open

The Waverley

You and I were new, drinking on the quay in the extended summer
when the Waverley steamer arrived.
It came in slowly, blocking Sheppey from view.

People looked up from pints and fish.
What is this?
Passengers photographed us and we photographed them.

We cooed and we clicked and we hugged each other.
Watched it dock.
Watched those waiting to get off.

Then, with the sea ahead, it continued its way.
The passengers felt closer this time.
They waved and we waved.

It grew smaller the further out –
that simultaneous feeling of regret and relief
when friends or visitors leave.

Each shingle-stone cast a shadow over the next shingle-stone
in a succession of shadows
and shingle-stones.

We walked home. I saw us –
two figures joined at the hands
with very long legs.

Notes

'...both ships and sea were things that broke to pieces' is from *The Harbours of England* by John Ruskin (1856).

'Bred in the Stone' uses lines from *Vanishing Cornwall* by Daphne Du Maurier (1967).

'The Penlee Lifeboat Disaster' is a found poem using voices from the BBC documentary *Cruel Sea: The Penlee Lifeboat Disaster,* which first aired 1st August 2006.

Acknowledgements

Acknowledgements are due to the journals *Ambit, PN Review,* and *Wild Court* where some of these poems have previously appeared.

Thanks are also due to Andy Brown, Rupert Loydell, André Naffis-Sahely, Declan Ryan, Michael Schmidt, and my tutors at The Poetry School.

My very special thanks to Aaron Kent, my parents and family, and Robert Selby.

LAY OUT YOUR UNREST